# Your guide to a Sound Mind

**KEEPING FAITH IN THE MIDST OF DARKNESS**

**JEREMY SHORTER**

www.JeremyShorter.net

*Your Guide To A Sound Mind*
Copyright © 2020 by Jeremy Shorter

No portion of this book may be reproduced, scanned, or distributed in any form without the written permission of the Author. Please purchase only authorized editions. For more information, please visit www.jeremyshorter.net.

**Copyright, Legal Notice, and Disclaimer:**
This publication is protected under the US Copyright Act of 1976 and all other application international, federal, state, and local laws, and All Rights Reserved, including resale.

Paperback ISBN: 978-0-578-80301-2
Hardback ISBN: 978-0-578-80581-8
eBook ISBN: 978-0-578-80302-9

Library of Congress Control Number: 2020922561

*Jeremy* SHORTER

www.jeremyshorter.net

# Preface

It is my prayer that this book will leave you with a sound mind and peace. Hopefully by reading these scriptures you will be encouraged and left with an understanding of how to endure tough situations. To be able to uplift someone's spirit or mend a broken heart by the words of The Most High God is a blessing in itself. My prayer and hope is that you will gain knowledge and understanding through The Most High God's words with confidence and faith, and not in fear. All scriptures will be given from the Authorized King James Version of the Bible, and the Apocrypha Authorized (King James) Version. For more information about me, visit www.JeremyShorter.net. In addition, I would like to thank The Most High God for feeding me with wisdom, knowledge, and understanding through his Son who is the Word.

**For I am persuaded, that neither death, nor life, nor angels, nor principalities, nor powers, nor things present, nor things to come, Nor height, nor depth, nor any other creature, shall be able to separate us from the love of God, which is in Christ Jesus our Lord.**

**Romans 8:38-39**

# Table of Contents

| | |
|---|---:|
| Faith | 1 |
| Endure | 8 |
| Death | 13 |
| Patience | 18 |
| Charity | 22 |
| Fear | 28 |
| Repentance | 32 |
| Humbleness | 35 |
| Prayer | 39 |
| Trusting in the Most High God | 42 |
| Forgiveness | 48 |
| Following The World | 53 |
| Children | 60 |
| Money | 68 |
| Worry & Stress | 74 |
| Fasting & Praying | 79 |
| Eating & Gluttony | 87 |
| Drinking & Wine | 90 |
| Men | 95 |
| Women | 102 |

# Faith

As children of The Most High God of Israel, we must learn to have faith in The Most High God of Israel. We, as children of The Most High God, must solely rely on the Holy One of Israel for everything. So, I say to you my brothers and sisters, have faith in The Most High God that he shall direct your paths. As the Word says, walk by Faith.

---

**Hebrews 11:1 Now, faith is the substance of things hoped for, the evidence of things not seen.**

The word of The Most High God says, "faith is the substance of things hoped for, and not seen"; so, have faith in The Most High God and not what you see, because what you see isn't always what it may seem to be. Walk as if you're a blind man and your guide is the Most High God.

---

**2 Peter 1:5-7 And beside this, giving all diligence, add to your faith virtue; and to virtue knowledge; And to knowledge temperance; and**

to temperance patience; and to patience godliness; And to godliness brotherly kindness; and to brotherly kindness charity.

We read that we must add to our "faith virtue and to virtue knowledge and to knowledge temperance and to temperance patience and to patience godliness and to godliness brotherly kindness and to brotherly kindness charity." All of these things will help us live a more righteous life and also help us walk more upright in the sight of The Most High God.

---

**1 John 5:4 For whatsoever is born of the Most High overcometh the world: and this is the victory that overcometh the world, even our faith.**

Those who are born of The Most High God, meaning those who are chosen by The Most High God as servants, will overcome the world. They will overcome the world by tribulation and persecution. Those who are walking upright in this world and believe in the Messiah will face challenges, but by having faith in The Most High God and trusting in Him you can overcome the wickedness of this world.

---

**Revelation 14:12 Here is the patience of the saints: here are they that keep the commandments of the Most High, and the faith of Jesus (Yashaya).**

**Saint**—A person of great holiness, virtue, or benevolence.

**Benevolence**—Inclination or tendency to help or do good to others; charity.

# FAITH

The Word of The Most High God says, "Here is the patience of the saints," and right after that it brings up a key point, "here are they that keep the commandments of the Most High." This is key because all those who are true saints of The Most High God will keep his commandments and follow after righteousness, and have faith in Jesus, whose name in Hebrew is Yashaya. So, walk upright in The Most High God and keep his laws, statutes, and commandments, and have faith in the Messiah who is the Son of God.

---

**Matthew 8:23-26 And when he was entered into a ship, his disciples followed him. And, behold, there arose a great tempest in the sea, insomuch that the ship was covered with the waves: but he was asleep. And his disciples came to him, and awoke him, saying, Lord, save us: we perish. And he saith unto them, Why are ye fearful, O ye of little faith? Then he arose, and rebuked the winds and the sea; and there was a great calm.**

His disciples in this situation had little faith and they feared; as fellow disciples of the Messiah, we must not show this same lack of faith at any situation that comes our way. That's why it's important for us to put all of our faith in The Most High God and trust in him with all our heart.

---

**Matthew 8:19-20 And a certain scribe came, and said unto him, Master, I will follow thee whithersoever thou goest. And Jesus (Yashaya) saith unto him, the foxes have holes, and the birds of the air have nests; but the Son of man hath not where to lay his head.**

The Messiah told of a certain scribe that came unto him and said, "I will follow thee wherever you go." Shortly after that the Messiah let him know by following him and denying himself that he must walk by faith and have faith in The Most High God. By following the Messiah and denying ourselves, we must understand that the world is going to hate us and cast our name down as evil for following the ways of the Messiah. We must have faith to truly and sincerely give our lives over to the Most High God through the Word, which is the Messiah.

---

**Romans 10:17 So then faith cometh by hearing, and hearing by the word of the Most High.**

We must understand that as believers in The Most High God of Israel, it's good to study the Word of The Most High God to increase our faith, but it's even better when we hear the Words of the Most High God from an elder or teacher of the Word.

---

**Luke 17:5-6 And the apostles said unto the Most High, Increase our faith. And the Lord said, If ye had faith as a grain of mustard seed, ye might say unto this sycamine tree, Be thou plucked up by the root, and be thou planted in the sea; and it should obey you.**

By having faith in The Most High God of Israel as a mustard seed, we will be able to do things and accomplish things that we never thought possible. When we put all of our faith in The Most High God, nothing is impossible.

---

**Romans 14:1 Him that is weak in the faith receive ye, but not to doubtful disputations.**

**Disputations**—The act or an instance of arguing.

# FAITH

Those that are weak in faith, meaning those who are weary in The Most High God, must be received without argument and confusion. Those who are servants of the Most High God must not strive with those who are weak in faith, but be gentle unto all men. Pray that The Most High God will give repentance to all who acknowledge the truth, as stated in 2 Timothy 2:24-26.

---

**2 Corinthians 5:7 For we walk by faith, not by sight.**

By trusting and believing in The Most High God of Israel we must not walk by sight, but faith alone. When we walk by faith and not by sight we allow ourselves to better fight against the enemy. As stated in Ephesians 6:12, "*for we wrestle not against flesh and blood, but against principalities, against powers, against the rulers of the darkness of this world, against spiritual wickedness in high places.*" We are fighting against an unseen enemy, yet by having faith in The Most High God, we can see the enemy devices.

---

**Galatians 5:22-23 But the fruit of the Spirit is love, joy, peace, long-suffering, gentleness, goodness, faith, Meekness, temperance: against such there is no law.**

As followers of Righteousness and believers of the God of Israel we must put on the fruits of the Spirit so that we can gain victory over the enemy through The Most High God.

---

# YOUR GUIDE TO A SOUND MIND

**Mark 11:22 And Jesus answering saith unto them, Have faith in God.**

The Messiah told us to have faith in his Father who is The Most High God of Israel. When we have faith in The Most High God we operate in a sound mind and allow the Holy Spirit to guide us in wisdom and understanding.

# Notes

# Endure

Having faith in The Most High God is good, but we must understand that we will go through much tribulation, as the scripture tells us in Acts 14:22. By knowing the tribulation and persecution that comes with following righteousness, we can accept that we have to endure all that comes our way. It's important to understand that enduring is key when we have faith in The Most High God of Israel. By believing in The Most High God's words we become enemies of the present world, thus causing the enemy to come and try to deceive us with his many devices. That's why we must endure and have faith in The Most High God.

---

**Matthew 24:13 But he that shall endure unto the end, the same shall be saved.**

Those who endure tribulation, persecution, and suffering for The Messiah's sake will be saved because they held their Faith.

---

**Mark 4:15-20 And these are they by the way side, where the word is sown; but when they have heard, Satan cometh immediately, and taketh away the word that was sown in their hearts. And these are they likewise which are sown on stony ground; who, when they have heard the word, immediately receive it with gladness; And have no root in themselves, and so endure but for a time: afterward, when affliction or persecution ariseth for the word's sake, immediately they are offended. And these are they which are sown among thorns; such as hear the word, And the cares of this world, and the deceitfulness of riches, and the lusts of other things entering in, choke the word, and it becometh unfruitful. And these are they which are sown on good ground; such as hear the word, and receive it, and bring forth fruit, some thirtyfold, some sixty, and some an hundred.**

---

We don't want to be one of those who receives the word with joy, and endure but for a little time when persecution and affliction comes our way, as stated in Mark 4:16-17. We also don't want to be one of those who hear the word, but care for the things of this world, and the deceitfulness of riches, and the lusts of other things because this chokes the word, and it becomes unfruitful, as shown in Mark 4:18-19. We want to be the ones that are sown on good ground so we can endure and walk by faith and believe in The Most High God of Israel.

---

**Mark 13:13 And ye shall be hated of all men for my name's sake: but he that shall endure unto the end, the same shall be saved.**

When you give your life over to The Most High God with a sincere heart, in a world filled with darkness, you will go through things just like the Messiah and the disciples. Please know that you are not alone, and realize that it is a blessing because you are partaking in Christ's suffering. When you go through these things you must endure till the end, meaning until death.. So fight the good fight of Faith.

---

**2 Timothy 2:1-3 Thou therefore, my son, be strong in the grace that is in Christ Jesus. And the things that thou hast heard of me among many witnesses, the same commit thou to faithful men, who shall be able to teach others also. Thou therefore endure hardness, as a good soldier of Jesus Christ.**

As followers of the Word (Christ) we must be strong and endure hardship as a good solider. What is the hardship you ask? The hardship that you must endure is the affliction, persecution, and suffering you must go through as a true follower of the Messiah in this present world filled with evil.

---

**2 Timothy 4:5 But watch thou in all things, endure afflictions, do the work of an evangelist, make full proof of thy ministry.**

**Affliction—** A condition of great distress, pain, or suffering.

As we read in 2 Timothy 4:5, we must endure afflictions. As already stated, when you give your life over to The Most High God with a sincere heart and turn towards righteousness to follow the Word (Christ) you will go through troubles, but know this, your rewards await you if you endure until the end.

---

# ENDURE

**Ecclesiasticus 2:2 Set thy heart aright, and constantly endure, and make not haste in time of trouble.** – *Authorized KJV Apocrypha*

**Constantly**— Continual or continuous.

**Haste**—To hurry; rush.

As the scripture tells us in the *KJV Bible*, we must set our hearts aright, meaning we must repent and confess our sins towards The Most High God. We should turn away from our wicked ways and keep the laws, statutes, judgments, and commandments of The Most High God of Israel. Then we must constantly endure and make not haste in the time of trouble, meaning we should not be so quick to run away when trouble comes our way, as the parables tells us in Mark 4:15-19.

# Notes

# Death

We must understand that death is a part of life, but by believing and having faith in The Most High God, we can get through any situation. Death is unexpected and when it comes your way, you must operate in wisdom and understanding to know how to deal with it.

---

**Hebrews 9:27 And as it is appointed unto men once to die, but after this the judgment.**

The Word of The Most High God says, man is appointed only once to die. You only get one chance to die. Please don't allow the enemy to fool you and to trick you into thinking that you can come back as someone else. Do not allow the enemy to make you believe in reincarnation. There is no such thing as reincarnations; you only die one time.

---

**Psalms 68:20 He that is our God is the God of salvation; and unto God the Lord belong the issues from death.**

# YOUR GUIDE TO A SOUND MIND

As we have just read in Psalms 68:20, the issues of death come from The Most High God of Israel. This is why you must operate with wisdom and understanding, because you don't want to allow the enemy to make you think that it's your fault or someone else's. It's up to The Most High God when someone dies.

---

**Ecclesiasticus 14:18 As of the green leaves on a thick tree, some fall, and some grow; so is the generation of flesh and blood, one cometh to an end, and another is born.** – *Authorized KJV Apocrypha*

Life must come to an end (Death), but know that when a man's, woman's, child's, or baby's life has to come to an end, another life is being born. Once you see that then you will be able to understand and see the blessing that comes with Death.

---

**Ecclesiasticus 41:3-4 Fear not the sentence of death, remember them that have been before thee, and that come after; for this is the sentence of the Lord over all flesh." And why art thou against the pleasure of the most High? There is no inquisition in the grave, whether thou have lived ten, or an hundred, or a thousand years.** – *Authorized KJV Apocrypha*

**Inquisition**— The act of inquiring deeply or searchingly; investigation.

We are commanded, yet again, to not fear the sentence of death. Death is according to The Most High God for he is righteous in all of his ways. As stated in Revelation 21:8, the fearful shall have their part in the lake of fire. What we must also understand is that sickness, disease, and other health related problems could be a result of sin. That's why it's important for everyone to confess their sins and repent with a sincere heart and follow after the Word (Christ).

---

**Ecclesiasticus 38:18-23 For of heaviness cometh death, and the heaviness of the heart breaketh strength. In affliction also sorrow remaineth: and the life of the poor is the curse of the heart. Take no heaviness to heart: drive it away, and member the last end. Forget it not, for there is no turning again: thou shalt not do him good, but hurt thyself. Remember my judgment: for thine also shall be so; yesterday for me, and to day for thee. When the dead is at rest, let his remembrance rest; and be comforted for him, when his Spirit is departed from him.** – *Authorized KJV Apocrypha*

When someone dies and you continually mourn for them, you will bring heaviness to your heart and that's not good. As stated in the above scripture, we must drive heaviness away from our hearts, for if we continue to have heaviness in our hearts for those that have died we will, in turn, hurt ourselves.

---

**Ecclesiasticus 33:23 At the time when thou shalt end thy days, and finish thy life, distribute thine inheritance.** – *Authorized KJV Apocrypha*

It is commanded that when a man is about to die, he is appointed to distribute his inheritance to his children or other family members.

---

**Ecclesiasticus 22:11-12 Weep for the dead, for he hath lost the light: and weep for the fool, for he wanteth understanding: make little weeping for the dead, for he is at rest: but the life of the fool is worse than**

**death. Seven days do men mourn for him that is dead; but for a fool and an ungodly man all the days of his life.** – *Authorized KJV Apocrypha*

We are commanded to weep for the dead for seven days, and if a man continues after that then they are considered a fool. Why? Because when you allow yourself to have a heavy heart, the enemy (Satan) can use that against you, thus causing you to lose faith and turn towards wickedness.

# Notes

# Patience

Patience is very important when serving The Most High God of Israel. Without patience, how can a man endure until the end? Having patience is a must if you plan on having faith in The Most High God. When you have patience you allow The Most High God to do what he needs to do for your situation. If you don't have patience, you will become weary and lose faith. So, be patient when you're facing challenges because The Most High God knows what you already need.

---

**Romans 5:3-5 And not only so, but we glory in tribulations also: knowing that tribulation worketh patience; And patience, experience; and experience, hope: And hope maketh not ashamed; because the love of God is shed abroad in our hearts by the Holy Ghost, which is given unto us.**

We must understand that tribulation brings out patience. You will learn that the experiences you go through will humble you and allow you to have patience in The Most High God, for he is Faithful and True.

# PATIENCE

**Romans 15:4 For whatsoever things were written aforetime were written for our learning, that we through patience and comfort of the scriptures might have hope.**

The Word of The Most High God says the things that were written before our time were written for our learning. All the stories in the Old Testament were written so that we might have patience in whatever situation we are going through, because there is nothing new under the sun.

---

**1 Timothy 6:11 But thou, O man of the Most High, flee these things; and follow after righteousness, godliness, faith, love, patience, meekness.**

We read in 1 Timothy 6:11 that patience is a form of righteousness. When you have patience you are showing your faith towards The Most High God and you are also showing your trust in Him (The Most High God).

---

**Hebrews 6:11-12 And we desire that every one of you do show the same diligence to the full assurance of hope unto the end: That ye be not slothful, but followers of them who through faith and patience inherit the promises.**

We are to show the same diligence as the former prophets and those who were followers of the Messiah until the end. We are to follow those who inherit the promises of Abraham, Isaac, and Jacob with faith and patience. Patience is what we need in order to get into the Kingdom of The Most High God. So have patience in your situation and pray without ceasing.

# YOUR GUIDE TO A SOUND MIND

---

**James 1:3-4 Knowing this, that the trying of your faith worketh patience. But let patience have her perfect work, that ye may be perfect and entire, wanting nothing.**

We just read that the trying of our "faith worketh patience;" therefore, we must be patient with whatever trials come our way, for we are to put our trust in The Most High God, and not man. Ware to "let patience have her perfect work," meaning let the Most High God deal with the situation at hand so that everything can go according to the will of The Most High God, and not what you desire should be done.

---

**Hebrews 10:36 For ye have need of patience, that, after ye have done the will of the Most High, ye might receive the promise.**

As followers of the Word (Christ), we have need of patience, but why? Because when we truly give our life over to The Most High God, we will have to go through adversity for the Word's sake. As you do the will of The Most High God you will need patience so that you may receive the promise. What is the promise? The promise is to inherit the Kingdom of Heaven and to have everlasting life.

# Notes

# Charity

We must examine ourselves to the full, as the Words of the Most High God have said. We must learn to do much charity work with a pure heart. Doing charity work is how we can learn to love one another and become the man or woman that The Most High God has ordained us to be. Also, charity covers a multitude of sin when you operate with a sincere heart. Love is Charity.

---

**1 Corinthians 13:3-8** And though I bestow all my goods to feed the poor, and though I give my body to be burned, and have not charity, it profiteth me nothing. Charity suffereth long, and is kind; charity envieth not; charity vaunteth not itself, is not puffed up, Doth not behave itself unseemly, seeketh not her own, is not easily provoked, thinketh no evil; Rejoiceth not in iniquity, but rejoiceth in the truth; Beareth all things, believeth all things, hopeth all things, endureth all things. Charity never faileth: but whether there be prophecies, they shall fail; whether there be tongues, they shall cease; whether there be knowledge, it shall vanish away.

# CHARITY

Let us put forth Charity and love rather than hate, envy and jealously. We must learn to walk in Charity towards our enemy if we are true followers of the Word (Christ). Charity suffereth long, it's kind, it's not envious, it does not brag (vaunteth), it's not arrogant or prideful, it doesn't behave itself inappropriately, doesn't seek its own way, is not provoked, it takes no account of evil, and charity (love) never fails. Rather than not helping one another reach our full potential that The Most High God has called us to be, let us examine ourselves so that we may be humble and walk more in love towards one another.

---

**1 Corinthians 13:11-13 When I was a child, I spake as a child, I understood as a child, I thought as a child: but when I became a man, I put away childish things. For now we see through a glass, darkly; but then face to face: now I know in part; but then shall I know even as also I am known. And now abideth faith, hope, charity, these three; but the greatest of these is charity.**

We read that the greatest of these is charity, which is love. Walking in love is the most gratifying thing you can do towards your fellow brother, sister and your enemy. When you operate in love you're operating in strength because it takes strength to forgive someone who has done evil towards you.

---

**1 Corinthians 14:1 Follow after charity, and desire spiritual gifts, but rather that ye may prophesy.**

The scripture tells us to "follow after charity" (love), no matter what someone does to offend us. As the Word of The Most High God says, love covers all sin. So, follow after charity in every situation.

**1 Corinthians 16:14 Let all your things be done with charity.**

Whatever you do for someone, you are to do it with charity (love). Doing things with love and a pure heart is the most gratifying feeling that a person can feel. Doing things with charity allows us to be humble and build up our faith. If you truly forgive someone, then do so out of charity (love). Don't allow the enemy (Satan) to get into your heart and cause you to hold a grudge, thus not allowing you to heal from the situation.

---

**Colossians 3:12-14 Put on therefore, as the elect of God, holy and beloved, bowels of mercies, kindness, humbleness of mind, meekness, longsuffering; Forbearing one another, and forgiving one another, if any man have a quarrel against any: even as Christ forgave you, so also do ye. And above all these things put on charity, which is the bond of perfectness.**

We are to walk and put on the things of the elect of The Most High God. Embrace love, for it is the only way we may be completely joined together.

---

**1 Timothy 1:5-7 Now the end of the commandment is charity out of a pure heart, and of a good conscience, and of faith unfeigned: From which some having swerved have turned aside unto vain jangling; Desiring to be teachers of the law; understanding neither what they say, nor whereof they affirm.**

We are commanded to walk in charity with a pure heart, a good conscience, and of faith unfeigned. So, whatever you're going through with somebody, walk in charity towards them with a pure heart so that you can humble yourself, and The Most High God will help you in your situation.

# CHARITY

**1Timothy 4:12-13 Let no man despise thy youth; but be thou an example of the believers, in word, in conversation, in charity, in spirit, in faith, in purity. Till I come, give attendance to reading, to exhortation, to doctrine.**

We are to be an example to those who don't have faith. As followers of the Word (Christ) we are not supposed to use curse words, raise our voices, or be quick to anger. Our conversations need to be carried out with Charity (love), and we should not try to prove a point or prove someone wrong. We should speak and hold a conversation out of love with hope and prayer that The Most High God will shed light upon them.

**2 Timothy 2:22 Flee also youthful lusts: but follow righteousness, faith, charity, peace, with them that call on the Lord out of a pure heart.**

We are told to flee youthful lusts, which bring evil and wicked spirits upon us, thus causing the enemy to use things against us so we can self-destruct and engulf ourselves in sin. We are told to follow after righteousness, and charity is a form of righteousness born out of a pure heart.

**Titus 2:1-5 But speak thou the things which become sound doctrine: That the aged men be sober, grave, temperate, sound in faith, in charity, in patience. The aged women likewise, that they be in behaviour as becometh holiness, not false accusers, not given to much wine, teachers of good things; That they may teach the young women to be sober, to love their husbands, to love their children, To be discreet,**

**chaste, keepers at home, good, obedient to their own husbands, that the word of God be not blasphemed.**

The aged men and woman are to walk in charity (love) towards the youth, which is the younger generation. If the older generation doesn't walk in charity (love) then how can they walk in love towards their fellow brothers and sisters, and for that matter, how can they learn to forgive one another?

---

**1 Peter 4:8 And above all things have fervent charity among yourselves: for charity shall cover the multitude of sins.**

We are commanded to have fervent charity among ourselves. When we walk with love and forgive our enemies who have come up against us, our sins are forgiven. However, we must forgive out of charity (love) and with a pure heart. If we want to build our faith and get deliverance over any situation, then we must sincerely, out of a pure heart walk in charity and love.

# Notes

# Fear

Fear is the main thing that the enemy uses against us to keep us away from the Most High God. Fear is of Satan, and not The Most High God. How can we say we love Christ when the scripture tells us in 1 John 4:18 "that there is no fear in love?" We can't serve the Messiah with fear. We must serve the Most High God with a sincere heart and without fear, because all those who are fearful will be thrown in the lake of fire. So let us not fear, because the Most High God didn't give us a spirit of fear, but rather a sound mind to operate in his wisdom and understanding.

**Fear**—To be afraid to do something, or of a person or thing; dread.

---

**Psalms 119:39 Turn away my reproach, which I fear: for thy judgments are good.**

**Reproach**— Something that causes or merits blame, rebuke, or disgrace.

David was asking The Most High God of Israel to turn away his reproach, which he fears. If we say we have faith in The Most High God then let us put our whole heart into believing and calling on The Most High God who is our Father. Whatever you may be going through right now, put it in the hands of The Most High God and pray unto him, and fear nothing. Know that everything will be okay.

---

**Proverbs 29:25 The fear of man bringeth a snare: but whoso putteth his trust in the LORD shall be safe.**

**Snare—** To catch or trap in, or as if in a snare; capture by trickery.

"The fear of man bringeth a snare" upon those who fear what man can and will do unto them. We are not to walk in fear of man, if we trust and believe in The Most High God. Fearing in man or anything else lets us know that our faith in The Most High God is not as strong as it should be.

**Luke 12:4-5 And I say unto you my friends, Be not afraid of them that kill the body, and after that have no more that they can do. But I will forewarn you whom ye shall fear: Fear him, which after he hath killed hath power to cast into hell; yea, I say unto you, Fear him.**

The Word of The Most High God says we are not to fear those who have the power to kill the body, meaning man. Whatever situation you are going through, just pray and fast, and let The Most High God deal with it. So again, don't fear what man can do unto the flesh, but rather fear The Most High God of Israel.

---

**Romans 8:15 For ye have not received the spirit of bondage again to fear; but ye have received the Spirit of adoption, whereby we cry, Abba, Father.**

The Word of The Most High God says we haven't received a spirit of bondage again to fear. So let us not walk in fear of what man can do unto us, or let us not walk in fear of any situation, but rather let us walk in faith trusting in The Most High God with all of our hearts. For The Most High God loves you and wants to see you reach the full potential of what he has called you to do.

---

**1 John 4:18 There is no fear in love; but perfect love casteth out fear: because fear hath torment. He that feareth is not made perfect in love.**

**Torment—** Physical or Mental pain.

"There is no fear in love," which is charity, "for charity casteth out fear". As we read in the previous chapter, charity is love. How can a man proclaim to have faith and serve The Most High God if he lives in fear or fears anything? The Word says fear has torment and we know that The Most High God doesn't deal with torment, for he loves all of those who sincerely love him and who serve him with a pure heart.

---

**Revelation 21:8 But the fearful, and unbelieving, and the abominable, and murderers, and whoremongers, and sorcerers, and idolaters, and all liars, shall have their part in the lake which burneth with fire and brimstone: which is the second death.**

Those who are full of fear and without faith will be cast into the lake of fire. It is important that we walk in faith, believing in The Most High God with all of our hearts. Being fearful is the opposite of having faith, so let us walk in faith and not fearing anything, for The Most High God is in charge of everything. Pray unto The Most High God and fast unto Him.

# Notes

# Repentance

It is very important for us to repent for the sins that we have committed. When you confess your sins with a sincere heart towards The Most High God, it is the first step of healing and allowing The Most High God to mold you into the man, woman, or child that you need to be. You must repent and turn away from your wicked ways so you can let your light shine before men so that they may glorify The Most High God.

---

**Baruch 2:12 O Lord our God, we have sinned, we have done ungodly, we have dealt unrighteously in all thine ordinances.** – *Authorized KJV Apocrypha*

We all have sinned before The Most High God of Israel. We have done ungodly things in the sight of The Most High God. Also, we have not kept his way, which is righteousness. That's why we are to repent for our sins, but this must be done with a sincere and pure heart.

---

# REPENTANCE

**1 John 3:4 Whosoever committeth sin transgresseth also the law: for sin is the transgression of the law.**

The Word says whoever commits a sin transgresses the laws of The Most High God. You may be asking yourself, what laws? As followers of the Word (Christ), we are to follow the laws, statutes, and the commandments of The Most High God. That's why we are to repent for sinning against the Holy Law of The Most High God.

---

**Psalms 38:17-18 For I am ready to halt, and my sorrow is continually before me. For I will declare mine iniquity; I will be sorry for my sin.**

**Halt**—To put an end (to something); stop.

We must sincerely pray unto The Most High God and repent for the sins we have done before him. So let us put an end to our sinning against The Most High God with prayers, and repent from our hearts.

---

**Psalms 32:5 I acknowledged my sin unto thee, and mine iniquity have I not hid. I said, I will confess my transgressions unto the LORD; and thou forgavest the iniquity of my sin. Selah.**

We are to repent to The Most High God for the sins we have committed before him, and we are to do so with a pure heart. We know that The Most High God forgave David of his sins, so repent unto The Most High God for the sins you have committed unto the Father.

# Notes

# Humbleness

Being humble is a must when it comes to enduring and getting through any situation. We must learn to put on the fruits of the spirit at all times and walk by faith. When you are humble you allow things to fall into their right place, without trying to correct the situation or problem through your emotions. We must learn to solely rely on The Most High God at all times and trust in him. To be humble is to see; when you are humble you see things better than when you're not humble. So let us humble ourselves in the sight of The Most High God and walk by Faith.

---

**Proverbs 22:4 By humility and the fear of the Most High are riches, and honor, and life.**

**Humility**—The state or quality of being humble.

Let us humble ourselves in the sight of The Most High God, for humility brings riches, honor, and life. So whatever your situation is in life, always remember to humble yourself and walk by faith, believing and trusting in The Most High God.

**2 Chronicles 7:14 If my people, which are called by my name, shall humble themselves, and pray, and seek my face, and turn from their wicked ways; then will I hear from heaven, and will forgive their sin, and will heal their land.**

If his people, the Children of Israel, who are the 12 Tribes, shall humble themselves and pray and seek him and turn away from their wicked ways, then he will hear them and forgive them of their sins, and will heal our land (Jerusalem). Also, those Gentiles who come and serve the Father must stay humble. So remember to always keep yourself humble no matter what situation you are in.

---

**Job 22:29 When men are cast down, then thou shalt say, There is lifting up; and he shall save the humble person.**

This scripture is what humbleness is all about, and it shows us that when men are in great distress or pain, The Most High God is there to deliver them. That's why it's important for all of us to humble ourselves, so that The Most High God can deliver us from our situation.

---

**Matthew 18:4 Whosoever therefore shall humble himself as this little child, the same is greatest in the kingdom of heaven.**

This explains a great feature that all us must display while serving The Most High God—we must humble ourselves as little children. Greatness in the kingdom of Heaven is not secured by seeking to be the greatest; in order to be great, you must humble yourself to obtain favor from The Most High God.

# HUMBLENESS

**James 4:6 But he giveth more grace. Wherefore he saith, the Most High resisteth the proud, but giveth grace unto the humble.**

**Grace**—Mercy; clemency.

The Most High God gives grace unto the humble person. The Most High God doesn't like prideful people, so humble yourself. If you are in a bad situation or going through something and feel there is no hope, have faith, pray and be humble.

---

**James 4:10 Humble yourselves in the sight of the Most High, and he shall lift you up.**

Let us humble ourselves in the sight of The Most High God through his Words, and let us also walk by faith, believing in Him for he shall never forsake those who love him.

---

**Ecclesiasticus 35:17 The prayer of the humble pierceth the clouds: and till it come nigh, he will not be comforted; and will not depart, till the Most High shall behold to judge righteously, and execute judgment.** – *Authorized KJV Apocrypha*

The prayers of those who are sincerely humble pierce the clouds until their prayer reaches the ears of The Most High God. The humble person shall be delivered from their situation, meaning they shall "be comforted."

# Notes

# Prayer

Prayer is a big part of enduring and having faith in The Most High God of Israel. One must understand the power of praying to The Most High God of Israel for deliverance from any situation. As stated in Galatian 4:26, we must pray towards the east, which is towards Jerusalem, the Mother of us all. We must learn to pray more and walk by faith. When we pray we are actually building our faith in The Most High God. So let us pray more and pray for our enemies.

---

**1 Kings 8:48-49 And so return unto thee with all their heart, and with all their soul, in the land of their enemies, which led them away captive, and pray unto thee toward their land, which thou gavest unto their fathers, the city which thou hast chosen, and the house which I have built for thy name: Then hear thou their prayer and their supplication in heaven thy dwelling place, and maintain their cause.**

**Matthew 6:6 But thou, when thou prayest, enter into thy closet, and when thou hast shut thy door, pray to thy Father which is in secret; and thy Father which seeth in secret shall reward thee openly. But**

when ye pray, use not vain repetitions, as the heathen do: for they think that they shall be heard for their much speaking. Be not ye therefore like unto them: for your Father knoweth what things ye have need of, before ye ask him.**

When you pray, go into a private place such as your closet, shut the door behind you, and pray unto The Most High God in secret; this will ensure that nobody can hear what you are praying for. Also, we are not to use "vain reputations," meaning we are not to talk as much, because The Most High God already knows what you are asking for, so pray unto The Father with a sincere heart.

---

**1 Thessalonians 5:17 Pray without ceasing.**

**Ceasing**—Without stopping; incessantly.

We are to "pray without ceasing," meaning we are to pray continually each and every day. Prayer is a must when it comes to believing and trusting in The Most High God.

---

**Ecclesiasticus 38:9 My son, in thy sickness be not negligent: but pray unto the Lord, and he will make thee whole.** – *Authorized KJV Apocrypha*

When we or someone we know are sick, we are told to pray unto The Most High God so that he may heal us and make us whole again. So, remember to pray for those who are sick, so that The Most High God can make you or someone else whole again.

# Notes

# Trusting in the Most High God

It's important that we trust in The Most High God at all times with a sincere heart. The Most High God is our refuge and we must trust in him, for he will direct our path when we come to him in prayer. Trusting in The Most High God is like crossing a minefield; it will give you an advantage over the enemy, and allow you to make sound judgment. We must learn to not put trust in man, but in The Most High God. For the Father (The Most High God) will direct your path in righteousness and not cause you to fail.

---

**2 Samuel 22:31 As for God, his way is perfect; the word of the Most High is tried: he is a buckler to all them that trust in him.**

The Most High God is a buckler to all of those who trust in him with a sincere heart, but not to those who doubt or to those with lukewarm faith. Let us be humble and place trust in The Most High God for he is faithful and true to his word.

# TRUSTING IN THE MOST HIGH GOD

**Psalms 4:5 Offer the sacrifices of righteousness, and put your trust in the Most High.**

Present your body as a living sacrifice of righteousness (Romans 12:1) and "put your trust in the Most High God." He will not forsake those who are sincerely seeking guidance.

---

**Psalms 34:22 The Most High redeemeth the soul of his servants: and none of them that trust in him shall be desolate.**

Those who put their trust in the Most High God will never be lead to destruction. The Father will deliver you out of your situation if you trust in him with your whole heart, not with a half heart or not with doubt, but only when you sincerely trust in him.

---

**Psalms 37:5 Commit thy way unto the Most High; trust also in him; and he shall bring it to pass.**

Commit your way unto The Most High God, and always trust in him. The problem or situation you are in may seem insurmountable, and you may feel like giving up, but remember to pray to The Most High God and put your full trust in him and he shall bring it to pass.

---

**Psalms 40:4 Blessed is that man that maketh the Most High his trust, and respecteth not the proud, nor such as turn aside to lies.**

When you put your trust in The Most High God you are blessed. Let us learn to trust in the Most High God, and not in this evil and wicked world like we have been tricked to do.

---

**Psalms 56:3-4 What time I am afraid, I will trust in thee. In the Most High I will praise his word, in the Most High I have put my trust; I will not fear what flesh can do unto me.**

Whenever you are afraid of the situation you are in, the disease that you have, or any other problem that you may be facing, put it in the hands of the Most High God by trusting in him and praying unto him, day and night, until you are made whole.

---

**Psalms 62:8 Trust in him at all times; ye people, pour out your heart before him: God is a refuge for us. Selah.**

You have to trust in the Most High God at all times. Don't just trust in him when things are going right, but rather put your trust in him when things aren't going right. Pour out your heart before him for he is our refuge. Truly the Most High God is our deliverance.

---

**Psalms 71:1 In thee, O LORD, do I put my trust: let me never be put to confusion.**

When you don't have your trust in the Most High God you will walk around with confusion at all times. So let us put our trust in him at all times as the Word of the Most High God has instructed us to do. When we trust in Him, we will have a sound mind, and not walk in confusion.

# TRUSTING IN THE MOST HIGH GOD

**Psalms 118:8 It is better to trust in the Most High than to put confidence in man.**

**Confidence—** A feeling of trust in a person or thing.

Why it's better to trust in the Most High God, you may ask? Putting your trust in man is like trusting a known theft with your money. Don't put your trust in man, put it in the Most High God who loves you as long as you love him and seek after his righteousness.

---

**Proverbs 29:25 The fear of man bringeth a snare: but whoso putteth his trust in the Most High shall be safe.**

Don't fear anything, for doing so will bring obstacles into your life. Those who put their trust in the Most High God with a sincere heart will be safe from all kinds of danger.

---

**Proverbs 30:5 Every word of the Most High is pure: he is a shield unto them that put their trust in him.**

The Most High God is faithful and true, so if you pray with a humble spirit and trust in Him, you have a shield of protection over you. He will never forsake you, so learn to trust in the Most High God.

---

**Nahum 1:7 The Most High is good, a strong hold in the day of trouble; and he knoweth them that trust in him.**

The Most High God is always good to us, as his children. We may not understand why things happen, and we may even get mad at the Father, but the Most High God is always good. When you are going through something, know that the Most High God will bring it to pass, for he knows those that trust in him.

---

**Proverbs 3:5 Trust in the Most High with all thine heart; and lean not unto thine own understanding.**

Trust in the Most High God with all of your heart. Do not doubt or be lukewarm. Trust only in the Most High God, for he shall show you the path to deliverance.

# Notes

# Forgiveness

When you believe and trust in The Most High God, one of the most important things to have is forgiveness. When you forgive your enemies or someone who has wronged you, the Father will forgive you as well. Forgiving is key when it comes to building your faith in The Most High God of Israel. Let us not keep what someone has done unto us in our hearts, for in doing so you will not be forgiven of the things you have done. Forgiveness is the healing process for you to move forward.

---

**Psalms 32:1 Blessed is he whose transgression is forgiven, whose sin is covered.**

Even the Most High God will forgive you of the transgressions that you have committed before him. If the Most High God can forgive, we too must also be able to forgive with a pure and sincere heart, so that we can move forward in life with a sound mind.

# FORGIVENESS

**Matthew 18:21-22 Then came Peter to him, and said, Lord, how oft shall my brother sin against me, and I forgive him? Till seven times? Jesus saith unto him, I say not unto thee, Until seven times: but, Until seventy times seven.**

Peter asked the Messiah, "How many times I shall forgive my brother who keeps sinning against me?" The Messiah answered and said, "Until seven times: but, until seventy times seven." We are to forgive those who have sinned against us no matter what the situation, and we are to forgive out of a sincere heart. Remember that forgiving someone doesn't mean that you have to trust them. The Word of the Most High God says, "Do good unto thy enemy, but don't trust your enemy." We must take that same wisdom and apply it with forgiveness.

**Luke 6:37-38 Judge not, and ye shall not be judged: condemn not, and ye shall not be condemned: forgive, and ye shall be forgiven: Give, and it shall be given unto you; good measure, pressed down, and shaken together, and running over, shall men give into your bosom. For with the same measure that ye mete withal it shall be measured to you again.**

We should not judge anyone for we are going to be judged. Likewise, we should not condemn or we too will be condemned. However, we must forgive so that we can be forgiven. You can't have resentment in your heart, for by doing so you allow the enemy (Satan) to corrupt you and your soul. So forgive out of a pure and sincere heart so the Most High God can forgive you as well.

---

**Ephesians 4:31-32 Let all bitterness, and wrath, and anger, and clamour, and evil speaking, be put away from you, with all malice: And be**

**ye kind one to another, tenderhearted, forgiving one another, even as God for Christ's sake hath forgiven you.**

Let us put away all the bad emotions that we may have, for they will bring about evil and wicked spirits. Let us put away all unrighteousness and let us walk in humbleness, faith and trust in the Most High God. Let us be kind one to another, tenderhearted, and forgiving, because the Most High God will forgive us if we come to him with a sincere heart, prayer, fasting, and repentance. So forgive those who have hurt you and walk in love and peace.

---

**Ecclesiasticus 28:2 Forgive thy neighbour the hurt that he hath done unto thee, so shall thy sins also be forgiven when thou prayest.** – *Authorized KJV Apocrypha*

Forgive your neighbors for any hurt that they have caused upon you and your family. Also, forgive those who have hurt you, so when you ask the Most High God for forgiveness, he will grant it because you have sincerely forgiven. Let us not walk with old eyes, but rather let us walk with new, spiritual eyes.

---

**Leviticus 19:18 Thou shalt not avenge, nor bear any grudge against the children of thy people, but thou shalt love thy neighbour as thyself: I am the LORD.**

**Grudge**—A persistent feeling of resentment, especially one due to some cause, such as an insult or injury.

Having a grudge is like trying to run up a hill with a computer on your back. Grudges damage and weaken your soul. Let us not grudge, but rather walk in love and peace towards our enemy, not trusting them but operating

## FORGIVENESS

in love. Don't allow the enemy into your heart, thus deceiving you, causing you to do something you will regret. Humble yourself and grudge not, and know that The Most High God will keep you safe.

---

**James 5:9 Grudge not one against another, brethren, lest ye be condemned: behold, the judge standeth before the door.**

Yet again the Words of The Most High God tell us not to hold a grudge against anyone. For if you have a grudge against someone, you will be judged by The Most High God and your sins won't be forgiven. Let us walk with a sincere heart towards those who have hurt us, not trusting in them, but walking in forgiveness.

# Notes

# Following The World

There are many people who love the things in this world and who are friends with the world. It is important to know the god of this world (Satan) wants you to serve him so he can pull you away from the Most High God who loves you. Following the ways of this world will lead you to hell, and that's why the scriptures tell us in Matthew 7:14: "Because strait is the gate, and narrow is the way, which leadeth unto life, and few there be that find it." Few find life because they are caught with the cares of this present world. They store up treasures here on earth and not in Heaven. So let us not follow the ways of this wicked world, but let us rather follow after The Most High God and everlasting life.

---

**James 4:4 Ye adulterers and adulteresses, know ye not that the friendship of the world is enmity with God? Whosoever therefore will be a friend of the world is the enemy of God.**

**Adulterer**—A person (Man) who has committed adultery.

**Adulteress**—A woman who has committed adultery.

If you are a follower of this wicked world, please humble yourself and pray unto the Most High God so that he may direct your path to live a righteous life, and not one fitted for destruction. Those who have committed adultery are enemies of the Most High God. Those who are friends with the world, and those who do such acts, can repent and ask for forgiveness out of a sincere heart and do it no more.

---

**Matthew 6:19-21 Lay not up for yourselves treasures upon earth, where moth and rust doth corrupt, and where thieves break through and steal: But lay up for yourselves treasures in heaven, where neither moth nor rust doth corrupt, and where thieves do not break through nor steal: For where your treasure is, there will your heart be also.**

**Treasure—** (1) A thing or person that is highly prized or valued. (2) To store up and save; hoard.

We are commanded to lay up our treasure in heaven; however, if we lay up treasure here on earth, thieves break in and steal it. Those who love this world and the things in it should think twice because they will begin to put their trust in man and their hearts will be corrupted. So, let us not store up treasure here on earth, but only in Heaven. Let your treasure be living a righteous life for the Most High God of Israel.

---

**Romans 12:2 And be not conformed to this world: but be ye transformed by the renewing of your mind, that ye may prove what is that good, and acceptable, and perfect, will of God.**

**Conformed—** To make or become similar in character or form.

## FOLLOWING THE WORLD

We are told to not to be like this evil and wicked world, because it will lead us to hell and darkness, no matter how much money one possesses. You must transform your mind from the carnal way of thinking to a more spiritual way. So, repent, humble yourself, pray, and fast before the Most High God so that he may deliver you out of this wicked world. Pray continually and consistently each day.

---

**1 John 2:15-17 Love not the world, neither the things that are in the world. If any man love the world, the love of the Father is not in him. For all that is in the world, the lust of the flesh, and the lust of the eyes, and the pride of life, is not of the Father, but is of the world. And the world passeth away, and the lust thereof: but he that doeth the will of God abideth for ever.**

**Love—** (1) To have a great attachment to and affection for. (2) Wholehearted liking for or pleasure in something.

If you love this world and the things that are in it, then the love of the Most High God is not in you. How can this be? When you love this world, how can you please the Most High God? When you love something you try to please it. How can you be friends with this wicked world and love the Most High God? You can't do that, because it means you are being lukewarm (Revelation 3:16). All that is in the world is only temporary, but those that are doing the will of the Most High God, day and night, fighting the good fight of faith, will abide forever. Those that do the will of the Most High God will, therefore, enter into the kingdom of Heaven. So, follow not this world for it will corrupt you.

---

**Mark 4:18-19 And these are they which are sown among thorns; such as hear the word, And the cares of this world, and the deceitfulness of**

riches, and the lusts of other things entering in, choke the word, and it becometh unfruitful.

Those who are sown among thorns and a stony ground (those who are lukewarm) trying to serve the Most High God will hear the word and all that it has to say; they will "choke the word," meaning they won't understand it and the Word will become of no value to them. As a result, they won't follow the Word of the Most High God, but instead they will follow after this wicked world. Please don't follow the ways of this world. Those who are struggling with following the ways of the world must pray. Do so and the Most High God shall deliver you from it.

---

**Mark 8:36-37 For what shall it profit a man, if he shall gain the whole world, and lose his own soul? Or what shall a man give in exchange for his soul?**

There are many who are involved in sports, entertainment, music, and even those on corporate levels, who have sold their soul to gain the things of this world. They have given their soul over to the enemy (Satan) for material pleasures, women, fame and riches (money). If this is you, please repent and ask the Most High God to deliver you from the snares of the enemy. Remember to pray without ceasing.

---

**1 Corinthians 3:19 For the wisdom of this world is foolishness with God. For it is written, He taketh the wise in their own craftiness.**

**Foolishness—** (1) Ridiculous or absurd; not worthy of consideration. (2) Unwise; silly.

# FOLLOWING THE WORLD

Those who are followers of this world will operate and speak like this world; the wisdom of this world is foolishness to the Most High God. The elders need not to try to lead and teach the young generation from the ways of this world, but rather teach them of the Word of the Most High God as it is written. So don't listen to the wisdom of this world, but be vigilant to what is going on around you so you won't be deceived by it. Listen to the voice of the Most High God so he can direct your path and keep you from all dangers.

---

**2 Corinthians 4:3-4 But if our gospel be hid, it is hid to them that are lost: In whom the god of this world hath blinded the minds of them which believe not, lest the light of the glorious gospel of Christ, who is the image of God, should shine unto them.**

You see when you don't really have faith in the Most High God, but you have faith and love the material things of this world, you allow Satan to blind your mind, causing you to live a sinful life before the Most High God. That's why it's important to not follow after this world; stop trying to fit in, but rather fit in into Christ's army and fight the good fight of faith. If you pray and fast with a sincere heart towards the Most High God, know that He will shine his glorious light on you to show you the truth.

---

**Job 9:24 The earth is given into the hand of the wicked: he covereth the faces of the judges thereof; if not, where, and who is he?**

If you know that our present world is given into the hand of the wicked, meaning Satan and his followers, then why are you trying to follow after its ways, especially if you know what's going on? Please be reminded that the god of this present world is Satan: He has the power to give and take, but remember it's only temporary, meaning it doesn't last. Serve the living God of Israel with all your heart.

---

**1 Timothy 6:7 For we brought nothing into this world, and it is certain we can carry nothing out.**

We brought nothing into this world, so let us not love or store treasure in this world. Once we die we can't carry anything with us, so why sell your soul for only temporary things? Store treasure in Heaven and follow after it; let us not cherish the things of this world, but cherish righteousness.

# Notes

# Children

According to the Word of The Most High God, it is very important for parents to know how to deal with their children. Just as The Most High God deals with us as his children, it's important to deal with our children in that same manner. As you read this study lesson, you will see that you are not to be a friend to your child. Parents often mistake chastisement as bad, but as you read the Word you will see that The Most High God only chastises those whom he loves. As stated in Hebrews 12:6, "For whom the Lord loveth he chasteneth, and scourgeth every son whom he receiveth."

---

**Ecclesiasticus 7:23-25 Hast thou children? Instruct them, and bow down their neck from their youth. Hast thou daughters? Have a care of their body, and shew not thyself cheerful toward them. Marry thy daughter, and so shalt thou have performed a weighty matter: but give her to a man of understanding.** – *Authorized KJV Apocrypha*

If you have children, instruct them in the wisdom of the Most High God and not after the ways of this world. If you have a daughter, make sure she covers her body up. Also, you are to marry your daughter over to a man of understanding and wisdom from the Most High God. Children obey your parents, and daughters cover your bodies and walk as the virtuous women of *The Bible* did, so that you can please the Most High God.

---

**Proverbs 13:24 He that spareth his rod hateth his son: but he that loveth him chasteneth him betimes.**

**Chasteneth**—To discipline or correct by punishment.

---

Those that don't chastise their children don't love their children. Those who chastise their children love them because they want the best for them and want to correct their wrong ways. Just like the Most High God chastises us as his children, we are to do the same thing. Also, children be happy that your parents chastising you, for they love you.

---

**Proverbs 22:15 Foolishness is bound in the heart of a child; but the rod of correction shall drive it far from him.**

Foolishness is in the heart of your children because they are young and have to learn wrong from right, but if you chastise them and correct their ways it will drive foolishness away from their heart. As the word says, hold your child to labor. Children, try not to walk in foolishness, but rather walk in knowledge and understanding.

---

**Proverbs 23: 13-14 Withhold not correction from the child: for if thou beatest him with the rod, he shall not die. Thou shalt beat him with the rod, and shalt deliver his soul from hell.**

The Word tells us to not to withhold correction from our children for chastisement is love. When a child is left without chastisement they will become disobedient and follow the ways of this world, thus causing them to be delivered to hell by their sins. As the word says, the wage of sin is death.

---

**Proverbs 29:15 The rod and reproof give wisdom: but a child left to himself bringeth his mother to shame.**

When you chastise your child and reprove them of their wrongdoing, you will allow wisdom to filter into their soul so that they can walk in knowledge and not the ways of this world. When children are left to themselves to think and behave, they will bring their mother and family to shame. Please don't allow the world to raise your children, for this world will lead your children to destruction. Correct your child and be not your child's friend for that will cause you to have a heavy heart. Children, please listen to your parents, as they want the best for you, but pray unto the Most High God for wisdom as instruction.

---

**2 Corinthians 12:14 Behold, the third time I am ready to come to you; and I will not be burdensome to you: for I seek not yours, but you: for the children ought not to lay up for the parents, but the parents for the children.**

## CHILDREN

Children are not to lay up an inheritance for their parents, but rather parents are to store up an inheritance for their children as the Word of the Most High God instructs.

---

**Ephesians 6:4 And, ye fathers, provoke not your children to wrath: but bring them up in the nurture and admonition of the Lord.**

**Provoke**—To cause to act or behave in a certain manner; incite or stimulate.

Fathers please don't provoke your children to wrath or anger because it will discourage them (Colossians 3:21). We are instructed to guide and nurture our children in the ways of the Most High God. Children must listen to their parents and not provoke their parents to have heavy hearts for their foolishness.

---

**Proverbs 22:6 Train up a child in the way he should go: and when he is old, he will not depart from it.**

When you train a child in their youth about morals and the ways of the Most High God, and you keep training them in wisdom, knowledge, and understanding of the Word of the Most High God, they will not depart away from it when they are older. This will allow them to teach their children the same that was taught to them, which should be by the Word of the Most High God. Children, please listen and humble yourself before your parents and receive their corrections and instructions.

---

**Ecclesiasticus-30-7-13** He that maketh too much of his son shall bind up his wounds; and his bowels will be troubled at every cry. An horse not broken becometh headstrong: and a child left to himself will be willful. Cocker thy child, and he shall make thee afraid: play with him, and he will bring thee to heaviness. Laugh not with him, lest thou have sorrow with him, and lest thou gnash thy teeth in the end. Give him no liberty in his youth, and wink not at his follies. Bow down his neck while he is young, and beat him on the sides while he is a child, lest he wax stubborn, and be disobedient unto thee, and so bring sorrow to thine heart. Chastise thy son, and hold him to labour, lest his lewd behaviour be an offence unto thee. – *Authorized KJV Apocrypha*

**Willful**— Intent on having one's own way; headstrong or obstinate.

**Cocker**— To pamper or spoil by indulgence.

**Follies**— A foolish action, mistake, idea, etc.

**Stubborn**— Refusing to comply, agree, or give in; obstinate.

As a parent, please do not make too much of your children to others, as doing so will hurt the children because now they have to keep up with a certain reputation that they may not want, thus causing them to be unhappy. Children that are left alone will want to have their way all the time, which can lead to disobedience. Many parents cocker (spoil) their children because they claim, "I want my child to have want I didn't have," or "I want a better life for them." What you, as a parent, must understand is that your life went that way according to the plan of the Most High God. So stop trying to spoil your child and be your child's friend because in the end you will be afraid of them. You will be afraid to say things back or correct them. Don't play with them all the time like you are their friend instead of their parent, because they will bring a heavy heart upon you

## CHILDREN

and cause sorrow through their actions. As a parent, don't always laugh at them, because doing so will lead you to a sad heart for them. Do not give children liberty when they are young, but rather hold them to doing things around the house as a job. Wink not at their follies (stupidity), but correct them immediately. We are to chastise our children by beating (wiping) them on the side so that they won't turn out to be stubborn and disobedient and bring sorrow into our hearts. Children obey and listen to your parents. Also read Deuteronomy 21:18-21.

**Ephesians 6:1-3 Children, obey your parents in the Lord: for this is right. Honour thy father and mother; (which is the first commandment with promise; That it may be well with thee, and thou mayest live long on the earth.**

**Obey**—To carry out (instructions or orders); comply with (demands).

Children, you are instructed to obey your parents in the sight of the Most High God, for this pleases the Most High God (Colossians 3:20). Parents, don't provoke your children to anger, because doing so will discourage them. Children, honor your father and mother so that you may live a long life upon earth.

---

**Matthew 15:4 For God commanded, saying, Honour thy father and mother: and, He that curseth father or mother, let him die the death.**

Children, honor your father and mother as it is written in the Word of the Most High God, for the child that curses or speaks evil of his father or mother shall not have a long life (Proverbs 20:20). No matter what your parents have done unto you, forgive them and pray for them. Parents humble yourself and walk in love towards your children. Also read Deuteronomy 27:16.

**Proverbs 28:24 Whoso robbeth his father or his mother, and saith, It is no transgression; the same is the companion of a destroyer.**

**Rob—** To take something from (someone) illegally, as by force or threat of violence.

Children, do not steal from your parents and tell yourself that you haven't done anything wrong, because you are in the same company of a destroyer, meaning a murderer. Children, learn to humble yourselves and work with your two hands and learn not to steal and take from your parents or anyone else. For the commandment says Thou shalt not steal (Exodus 20:15).

# Notes

# Money

Money has caused many people to err, and money has also destroyed many people's souls. The love of money is the root of all evil. Also, it is evil for a man to want to get rich quick. We are told by the Word of The Most High God to not labor to be rich. There are many women that desire to be with rich men, but what they must understand is that the rich men whom they lay with could be evil, thus making them turn from the ways of The Most High God. It is hard for rich men to enter into Heaven because they have polluted themselves with the things of this world and have not followed after righteousness. People who are rich or have some level of wealth must understand that they can't serve two masters; they can't serve The Most High God and money, because there will be more love for one over the other.

---

**Proverbs 23:4-5 Labour not to be rich: cease from thine own wisdom. Wilt thou set thine eyes upon that which is not? for riches certainly make themselves wings; they fly away as an eagle toward heaven.**

**Labour**—Productive work, especially physical toil done for wages.

# MONEY

Have you ever heard someone say, "I want to go to college so I can get this job and make this amount of money?" Well, the scripture tells us not to labor to be rich, and to "cease from thine own wisdom," meaning from worldly wisdom, which persuades men to use all possible means to get rich. So, let us not labor to be rich, but rather let us labor to be rich in the spirit of the Most High God.

---

**Proverbs 28:22 He that hasteth to be rich hath an evil eye, and considereth not that poverty shall come upon him.**

**Haste—** Make haste to hurry; rush.

Those of you who haste to be rich have an evil eye, and don't consider the poverty that shall come upon you. Instead of hasting to be rich, haste after righteousness and do the will of the Most High God.

---

**Matthew 19:23-24 Then said Jesus unto his disciples, Verily I say unto you, That a rich man shall hardly enter into the kingdom of heaven. And again I say unto you, It is easier for a camel to go through the eye of a needle, than for a rich man to enter into the kingdom of God. It is easier for a camel to go through the eye of a needle, than for a rich man to go through the strait gate: that is, humanly speaking, it is an absolute impossibility. Rich man! tremble! feel this impossibility; else thou art lost for ever!**

**Hardly—** Scarcely; barely.

Those who are rich shall hardly every enter into the kingdom of the Most High God. It is easier for a camel to go through the eye of a needle, than for a rich man to enter into the kingdom of God. So, if you are rich, humble yourself and help out the true servants of the Most High God by doing a lot of charity work. Also read Mark 10:25 and Luke 18:25.

---

**1 Timothy 6:9-10 But they that will be rich fall into temptation and a snare, and into many foolish and hurtful lusts, which drown men in destruction and perdition. For the love of money is the root of all evil: which while some coveted after, they have erred from the faith, and pierced themselves through with many sorrows.**

**Temptation**—The act of tempting or the state of being tempted.

**Snare**— Anything that traps or entangles someone or something unawares.

**Lusts**— (1) A strong desire for sexual gratification. (2) A strong desire or drive.

**Perdition**— A final and irrevocable spiritual ruin.

**Covet**— To wish, long, or crave for (something, especially the property of another person).

**Erred**— To stray from the right course or accepted standards; sin.

**Sorrows**— (1) The characteristic feeling of sadness, grief, or regret associated with loss, bereavement, sympathy for another's suffering, for an injury done, etc. (2) A particular cause or source of regret, grief, etc.

"They that will be rich, fall into temptation and a snare." They will also fall into many hurtful desires, which are sown and fed by having more than they need; these desires cause destruction to the body, and perdition for the soul. The love of money is the root, and parent, of all evil. Those who covet money miss the mark, for they aim not at faith, but at something else. The rich have pierced themselves with many sorrows such as a guilty conscience, tormenting passions, desires contrary to reason, religion, and many others. How cruel are worldly men to themselves?

---

**1 Timothy 6:17-18 Charge them that are rich in this world, that they be not high-minded, nor trust in uncertain riches, but in the living God, who giveth us richly all things to enjoy; That they do good, that they be rich in good works, ready to distribute, willing to communicate.**

**Charge—** To set or demand (a price).

**High-minded—**Arrogant; haughty.

**Distribute—** (1) To give out in shares; dispense. (2) To hand out or deliver.

Scriptures tell us to charge the rich in this world so they won't be high-minded. The rich need not to trust in uncertain riches that they can lose in an hour, but rather trust in the Most High God who gives to us all things freely and abundantly. We must make sure they do good, meaning we must give them a daily task as this is their daily employ that they may be rich and abound in all good works. The rich need to be ready to distribute to the people, and be willing to communicate and join in all public works of charity.

---

**Ecclesiasticus 31:1 Watching for riches consumeth the flesh, and the care thereof driveth away sleep.** – *Authorized KJV Apocrypha*

**Watchful—** not sleeping

Watching for riches consumes and destroys the flesh, and the care of it drives away sleep. We shouldn't be watching for riches, but instead serving the Most High in spirit and truth.

---

**Ecclesiasticus 30:14-17 Better is the poor, being sound and strong of constitution, than a rich man that is afflicted in his body. Health and good estate of body are above all gold, and a strong body above infinite wealth. There is no riches above a sound body, and no joy above the joy of the heart. Death is better than a bitter life or continual sickness. -** *Authorized KJV Apocrypha*

**Constitution—** A person's state of health.

It is better to be a poor man who is in good health and have a sound mind, than to be a rich man and in bad health. Money can't turn away sickness when it is from the Most High God; so let those who are rich humble themselves and seek after righteousness.

# Notes

# Worry & Stress

It is important to not worry or stress about anything, because that shows a lack of trust and faith in the Most High God. When you come to serve The Most High God with a sincere heart you will have to go through things, but the scriptures tell us to see it as joy for we are partaking in Christ's suffering. Worry and stress can cause you to be sick, and thus, allow the enemy to use his devices on you and cause you to lose faith in the living God who is The Most High God of Israel. Don't worry or stress about the things that you are going through, but rather pray towards the east and fast before The Most High God, so that he may hear your prayer and give you strength.

---

**Psalms 37:5 Commit thy way unto the LORD; trust also in him; and he shall bring it to pass.**

When you have faith and trust in the Most High God with all of your heart, he will bring it to pass. You have to learn to walk by faith and not what you see, because the enemy will put strong delusions before your face to deceive you and to make you think that there is no hope. So, remember to put your situation in the hands of the Most High God through prayer and fasting.

---

**Psalms 55:22 Cast thy burden upon the LORD, and he shall sustain thee: he shall never suffer the righteous to be moved.**

**Burden**— Something that is exacting, oppressive, or difficult to bear.

You must learn to cast your burdens on the Most High God so he can sustain you. You must not rely or trust in man, but rather pray and have faith in the Most High God. Don't allow stress to plague you, but rather pray without ceasing for deliverance over your situation.

**Romans 8:26-28 Likewise the Spirit also helpeth our infirmities: for we know not what we should pray for as we ought: but the Spirit itself maketh intercession for us with groanings which cannot be uttered. And he that searcheth the hearts knoweth what is the mind of the Spirit, because he maketh intercession for the saints according to the will of God. And we know that all things work together for good to them that love God, to them who are the called according to his purpose.**

**Infirmities**— Physical weakness or debility; frailty.

**Intercession**— The act of interceding or offering petitionary prayer to God on behalf of others.

In Romans 8:26 we see that the spirit of the Most High God helps our infirmity and makes intercession for us with groaning which can't be heard. That's why it's important for us to trust in the Most High God and have faith in him. Learn to pray and trust in the Most High God and know that the Most High God will heal you and bring your problems to pass, if you pray unto him day and night. So, don't worry, learn to humble yourself, and put it in the hands of the Most High God.

---

**Philippians 4:6-7 Be careful for nothing; but in every thing by prayer and supplication with thanksgiving let your requests be made known unto God. And the peace of God, which passeth all understanding, shall keep your hearts and minds through Christ Jesus.**

We are to let our requests be known to the Most High God because he cares for those who love him and seek after him with a sincere heart through prayer and being a doer of the Word. We are to pray unto the Father and ask for deliverance over our problems and our present situations. Remember, prayer changes things if you stay constant.

---

**Matthew 6:25-34 Therefore I say unto you, Take no thought for your life, what ye shall eat, or what ye shall drink; nor yet for your body, what ye shall put on. Is not the life more than meat, and the body than raiment? Behold the fowls of the air: for they sow not, neither do they reap, nor gather into barns; yet your heavenly Father feedeth them. Are ye not much better than they? Which of you by taking thought can add one cubit unto his stature? And why take ye thought for raiment? Consider the lilies of the field, how they grow; they toil not, neither do they spin: And yet I say unto you, That even Solomon in all his glory was not arrayed like one of these. Wherefore, if God so clothe the grass of the field, which to day is, and to morrow is cast into the oven, shall he not much more clothe you, O ye of little faith? Therefore take no thought, saying, What shall we eat? or, What shall we drink? or, Wherewithal shall we be clothed? (For after all these things do the Gentiles seek:) for your heavenly Father knoweth that ye have need of**

**all these things. But seek ye first the kingdom of God, and his righteousness; and all these things shall be added unto you. Take therefore no thought for the morrow: for the morrow shall take thought for the things of itself. Sufficient unto the day is the evil thereof.**

Learn to humble yourself and walk by faith and take no thought for your life; what we shall eat, what we shall drink, and what we shall put on. We are to trust in the Most High God with all of our hearts and we should trust in Him at all times. So, whatever you are going through right now pray unto him, with a sincere heart, with repentance, and he shall deliver you and bring your present problem to pass.

---

**1 Peter 5:7 Casting all your care upon him; for he careth for you.**

This scripture says it all: stop your worrying and stressing and know that the Most High God cares for you. Pray unto him with a sincere heart and know that he is there for you no matter what the world has you to think.

# Notes

# Fasting & Praying

Fasting and praying are very powerful towards the Most High God, and are also very good for your health. We must not just fast and pray to the Most High God when we need something or want deliverance out of a situation, but also when we are thankful and content. When you are fasting and praying you hear from the Most High God in a clearer voice. Fasting and praying allows your spiritual eyes to be open, and it also humbles you.

---

**1 Samuel 7:3-12 And Samuel spake unto all the house of Israel, saying, If ye do return unto the LORD with all your hearts, then put away the strange gods and Ashtaroth from among you, and prepare your hearts unto the LORD, and serve him only: and he will deliver you out of the hand of the Philistines. Then the children of Israel did put away Baalim and Ashtaroth, and served the LORD only. And Samuel said, Gather all Israel to Mizpeh, and I will pray for you unto the LORD. And they gathered together to Mizpeh, and drew water, and poured it out before the LORD, and fasted on that day, and said there, We have sinned against the LORD. And Samuel judged the children of Israel in Mizpeh.**

**And when the Philistines heard that the children of Israel were gathered together to Mizpeh, the lords of the Philistines went up against Israel. And when the children of Israel heard it, they were afraid of the Philistines. And the children of Israel said to Samuel, Cease not to cry unto the LORD our God for us, that he will save us out of the hand of the Philistines. And Samuel took a sucking lamb, and offered it for a burnt offering wholly unto the LORD: and Samuel cried unto the LORD for Israel; and the LORD heard him. And as Samuel was offering up the burnt offering, the Philistines drew near to battle against Israel: but the LORD thundered with a great thunder on that day upon the Philistines, and discomfited them; and they were smitten before Israel.**

**And the men of Israel went out of Mizpeh, and pursued the Philistines, and smote them, until they came under Bethcar. Then Samuel took a stone, and set it between Mizpeh and Shen, and called the name of it Ebenezer, saying, Hitherto hath the LORD helped us.**

When you pray and fast you will see the Most High God work. There was a time when the children of Israel were dealing with paganism and other gods, but they decided to turn away from their wickedness. In 1 Samuel 7:6 it says *"And they gathered together to Mizpeh, and drew water, and poured it out before the LORD, and fasted on that day, and said there, We have sinned against the LORD. And Samuel judged the children of Israel in Mizpeh."* So when they children of Israel wanted to repent from their sins and evil, they fasted. Also, notice that it said they drew water and poured it out, instead of drinking it. So when you have sinned before the Most High God and need deliverance out of a situation, pray and fast before the Most High God with a sincere heart so he can help you and bring your situation to pass.

2 Chronicles 20:1-23 It came to pass after this also, that the children of Moab, and the children of Ammon, and with them other beside the monites, came against Jehoshaphat to battle. Then there came some that told Jehoshaphat, saying, There cometh a great multitude against thee from beyond the sea on this side Syria; and, behold, they be in Hazazontamar, which is Engedi. And Jehoshaphat feared, and set himself to seek the LORD, and proclaimed a fast throughout all Judah. And Judah gathered themselves together, to ask help of the LORD: even out of all the cities of Judah they came to seek the LORD. And Jehoshaphat stood in the congregation of Judah and Jerusalem, in the house of the LORD, before the new court, And said, O LORD God of our fathers, art not thou God in heaven? And rulest not thou over all the kingdoms of the heathen? And in thine hand is there not power and might, so that none is able to withstand thee? Art not thou our God, who didst drive out the inhabitants of this land before thy people Israel, and gavest it to the seed of Abraham thy friend forever? And they dwelt therein, and have built thee a sanctuary therein for thy name, saying, If, when evil cometh upon us, as the sword, judgment, or pestilence, or famine, we stand before this house, and in thy presence, (for thy name is in this house,) and cry unto thee in our affliction, then thou wilt hear and help. And now, behold, the children of Ammon and Moab and mount Seir, whom thou wouldest not let Israel invade, when they came out of the land of Egypt, but they turned from them, and destroyed them not; Behold, I say, how they reward us, to come to cast us out of thy possession, which thou hast given us to inherit.

O our God, wilt thou not judge them? For we have no might against this great company that cometh against us; neither know we what to do: but our eyes are upon thee. And all Judah stood before the LORD, with their little ones, their wives, and their children. Then upon Jahaziel the son of Zechariah, the son of Benaiah, the son of Jeiel, the son of Mattaniah, a Levite of the sons of Asaph, came the

Spirit of the LORD in the midst of the congregation; And he said, Hearken ye, all Judah, and ye inhabitants of Jerusalem, and thou king Jehoshaphat, Thus saith the LORD unto you, Be not afraid nor dismayed by reason of this great multitude; for the battle is not yours, but God's. To morrow go ye down against them: behold, they come up by the cliff of Ziz; and ye shall find them at the end of the brook, before the wilderness of Jeruel. Ye shall not need to fight in this battle: set yourselves, stand ye still, and see the salvation of the LORD with you, O Judah and Jerusalem: fear not, nor be dismayed; to morrow go out against them: for the LORD will be with you. And Jehoshaphat bowed his head with his face to the ground: and all Judah and the inhabitants of Jerusalem fell before the LORD, worshipping the LORD. And the Levites, of the children of the Kohathites, and of the children of the Korhites, stood up to praise the LORD God of Israel with a loud voice on high.

And they rose early in the morning, and went forth into the wilderness of Tekoa: and as they went forth, Jehoshaphat stood and said, Hear me, O Judah, and ye inhabitants of Jerusalem; Believe in the LORD your God, so shall ye be established; believe his prophets, so shall ye prosper. And when he had consulted with the people, he appointed singers unto the LORD, and that should praise the beauty of holiness, as they went out before the army, and to say, Praise the LORD; for his mercy endureth forever. And when they began to sing and to praise, the LORD set ambushments against the children of Ammon, Moab, and mount Seir, which were come against Judah; and they were smitten. For the children of Ammon and Moab stood up against the inhabitants of mount Seir, utterly to slay and destroy them: and when they had made an end of the inhabitants of Seir, every one helped to destroy another.

We see that the Most High God heard the prayers of the 12 Tribes and told them they didn't need to fight for the battle that is not there. In verse

22 and 23, you will see that the Most High God defeated the enemies of Israel. Let us pray and fast before the Most High God in our situation so we to can have the same victory over whatever we are going through.

---

**Nehemiah 1:1-7 The words of Nehemiah the son of Hachaliah. And it came to pass in the month Chisleu, in the twentieth year, as I was in Shushan the palace, That Hanani, one of my brethren, came, he and certain men of Judah; and I asked them concerning the Jews that had escaped, which were left of the captivity, and concerning Jerusalem. And they said unto me, The remnant that are left of the captivity there in the province are in great affliction and reproach: the wall of Jerusalem also is broken down, and the gates thereof are burned with fire. And it came to pass, when I heard these words, that I sat down and wept, and mourned certain days, and fasted, and prayed before the God of heaven, And said, I beseech thee, O LORD God of heaven, the great and terrible God, that keepeth covenant and mercy for them that love him and observe his commandments: Let thine ear now be attentive, and thine eyes open, that thou mayest hear the prayer of thy servant, which I pray before thee now, day and night, for the children of Israel thy servants, and confess the sins of the children of Israel, which we have sinned against thee: both I and my father's house have sinned. We have dealt very corruptly against thee, and have not kept the commandments, nor the statutes, nor the judgments, which thou commandedst thy servant Moses.**

Jonah went to Ninveh and preached to the people and they repented and turned from their evil ways. As we read, we see that the Most High God was about to destroy Ninveh for their sins, and the people of Ninveh thought maybe if they fasted and prayed before the Most High God that he would bless them. That's exactly what he did, the Father blessed them. As we have read in these testimonies, when we fast and pray before the Most

High God with a sincere heart, He will deliver us out of our situation. Let go and trust in the Most High God of Israel.

---

**Daniel 9:2-5 In the first year of his reign I Daniel understood by books the number of the years, whereof the word of the LORD came to Jeremiah the prophet, that he would accomplish seventy years in the desolations of Jerusalem. And I set my face unto the Lord God, to seek by prayer and supplications, with fasting, and sackcloth, and ashes: And I prayed unto the LORD my God, and made my confession, and said, O Lord, the great and dreadful God, keeping the covenant and mercy to them that love him, and to them that keep his commandments; We have sinned, and have committed iniquity, and have done wickedly, and have rebelled, even by departing from thy precepts and from thy judgments: Neither have we hearkened unto thy servants the prophets, which spake in thy name to our kings, our princes, and our fathers, and to all the people of the land.**

Daniel prayed and fasted when he wanted understanding of a vision that he had about the destruction of Jerusalem. Once he prayed and fasted, the Most High God gave him revelation about that dream. Humble yourself and pray and fast before the Most High God, and he will always come through—no matter how long it takes, trust in Him.

---

**Tobit 12:8 Prayer is good with fasting and alms and righteousness. A little with righteousness is better than much with unrighteousness. It is better to give alms than to lay up gold:** – *Authorized KJV Apocrypha*

When you pray and fast you are denying yourself and taking your focus off what you want, and putting your attention and focus on what the Heavenly Father wants. Remove all of your doubt and humble yourself and put your faith and trust in the Most High God, for he is faith and truth. Pray and fast before the Most High God that you be delivered, and you too shall overcome.

# Notes

# Eating & Gluttony

Eating is a necessary part of everyday life, but it can be a problem if you eat too much. We must learn what foods are prescribed according to the Word of the Most High God. As pointed out in Leviticus 11:1-47, the Most High God tells us what animals we can and can't eat. Yes, we have a Holy dietary law that we are to follow as servants and followers of the Most High God. This is done to protect us from various diseases that come from unclean animals like pork, crab, and catfish. When we eat unclean food and meat we become sick and ill, so let us not eat unclean food and let us not be excessive when eating.

---

**Proverbs 23:20-21 Be not among winebibbers; among riotous eaters of flesh: For the drunkard and the glutton shall come to poverty: and drowsiness shall clothe a man with rags.**

**Glutton—** A person devoted to eating and drinking to excess; greedy person.

We are not to be around those who lust over food and become gluttons. If you have a strong appetite for food and love food, then pray unto the Most High God for deliverance to remove that desire. Know that those who are gluttons shall become poor.

---

**Proverbs 23:2 And put a knife to thy throat, if thou be a man given to appetite.**

Don't be quick to eat whatever you see; restrain from a strong appetite towards food. It is not good to have a strong appetite for food; instead have a strong appetite for righteousness and trust in the Most High God.

---

**Ecclesiasticus 37:29-30 Be not unsatiable in any dainty thing, nor too greedy upon meats: For excess of meats bringeth sickness, and surfeiting will turn into choler.** – *Authorized KJV Apocrypha*

**Greedy**—Excessively desirous of food or wealth, especially in large amounts; voracious.

Don't be greedy when it comes to food, and know that too much meat will bring about sickness. Don't be glutton when it comes to eating, because it's not a good thing. Pray to the Most High God and follow his righteous path.

# Notes

# Drinking & Wine

Drinking is common for people who try to forget about things that they have done, or who want to make themselves feel good for the moment. Being a drunkard is not a good thing, because it can result in serious health problems. Wine is considered healthy, but not in excess. Drink in moderation, and don't drink to make yourself feel good, for that will lead you to make excuses and then cover up the real problems that you have.

---

**Proverbs 23:20-21 Be not among winebibbers; among riotous eaters of flesh: For the drunkard and the glutton shall come to poverty: and drowsiness shall clothe a man with rags.**

**Winebibbers—** A person who drinks a great deal of wine.

**Drunkard—** Intoxicated with or as if with alcohol.

We are instructed not be around those who drink a lot of wine for they will come to poverty. If you have a problem with drinking too much wine, please pray to the Most High God to remove that taste from your mouth.

# DRINKING & WINE

**Proverbs 20:1 Wine is a mocker, strong drink is raging: and whosoever is deceived thereby is not wise.**

**Mocker**—To imitate, especially in fun; mimic.

Wine is a mocker, and beer (strong drink) is a brawler. Whoever is led astray by them is not wise. So pray unto the Most High God that he deliver you from your drinking problem. Pray and fast unto him and this too shall pass.

---

**Proverbs 21:17 He that loveth pleasure shall be a poor man: he that loveth wine and oil shall not be rich.**

He that love wine shall not be rich. Humble yourself and pray unto the Most High God to give you a strong heart to endure, and pray unto the Most High God day and night for deliverance over your problem. He will bring it to pass.

---

**Proverbs 31:6 Give strong drink unto him that is ready to perish, and wine unto those that be of heavy hearts.**

We are told to give strong drink to him who is ready to perish (die); and wine to the bitter soul. In certain situations it is okay to drink a strong drink or wine, but it must be done in moderation.

**Ecclesiasticus 19:2 Wine and women will make men of understanding to fall away: and he that cleaveth to harlots will become impudent.** – *Authorized KJV Apocrypha*

Wine and women will make a wise man fall away, meaning cause them to err. Please pay attention to how much wine you are drinking and don't fornicate when dealing with women and wine.

---

**Ecclesiasticus 31:25-31 Shew not thy valiantness in wine; for wine hath destroyed many. The furnace proveth the edge by dipping: so doth wine the hearts of the proud by drunkenness. Wine is as good as life to a man, if it be drunk moderately: what life is then to a man that is without wine? for it was made to make men glad. Wine measurably drunk and in season bringeth gladness of the heart, and cheerfulness of the mind: But wine drunken with excess maketh bitterness of the mind, with brawling and quarrelling. Drunkenness increaseth the rage of a fool till he offend: it diminisheth strength, and maketh wounds. Rebuke not thy neighbour at the wine, and despise him not in his mirth: give him no despiteful words, and press not upon him with urging him to drink.** – *Authorized KJV Apocrypha*

**Valiantness**— Courageous, intrepid, or stout-hearted; brave.

**Quarrelling**— An angry disagreement; argument.

Don't show how much wine you can drink, for wine has destroyed and caused the death of many. Wine is good if it is drunk in moderation, and wine that is drunk in season brings gladness of the heart and cheerfulness of the mind. Too much wine will make you bitter of the mind, and you will find yourself arguing and acting crazy. Drunkenness will increase the rage of a fool till someone gets hurt, which is what it means when the Word says, "it makes wounds." Also, drunkenness diminishes your strength. So, let us drink wine in moderation and obey the Word of the Most High God.

---

**Ecclesiasticus 40:20 Wine and music rejoice the heart: but the love of wisdom is above them both.** – *Authorized KJV Apocrypha*

Wine that is drunk in moderation and with music, rejoice the heart. This means that if you're at a party or gathering, it is okay to drink a little wine, as long as it's not done in excess. Remember to always think upon the Words of the Most High God to lead and guide you.

---

**1 Corinthians 6:9-10 Know ye not that the unrighteous shall not inherit the kingdom of God? Be not deceived: neither fornicators, nor idolaters, nor adulterers, nor effeminate, nor abusers of themselves with mankind, Nor thieves, nor covetous, nor drunkards, nor revilers, nor extortioners, shall inherit the kingdom of God.**

Those who are drunks will not inherit the Kingdom of the Most High God. So, if you have a drinking problem, whether you are a man or woman, pray and fast before the Most High God for deliverance, and ask Him to remove that drinking spirit out of you, so you can better serve Him in spirit and truth.

# Notes

# Men

As a man, and especially as a man of the Most High God, you have to be very careful of women. There are many men who have gone down the wrong path for a woman and died. Pray unto the Most High God that he lead you not to a wicked woman, but a woman ordained for you, if that's the Most High God's will. Also, we must learn to humble ourselves and not be moved by our emotions and our wants and desires. You must learn to trust and have patience for the Most High God that he will direct the right woman into your life.

---

**Proverbs 9:13 A foolish woman is clamorous: she is simple, and knoweth nothing.**

**Clamorous**—To make a loud noise or outcry; make a public demand.

Men, please stay away from a foolish and loud (clamorous) woman, for she is simple and knows nothing. If you have a woman like this and you love her, then pray unto the Most High God that he humbles her and allows her to see how a woman is supposed to be, according to the Word of the Most High God.

---

**Proverbs 21:9 It is better to dwell in a corner of the housetop, than with a brawling woman in a wide house.**

**Brawling—** A loud disagreement or fight.

Men, please stay away from a woman who likes to cause unwanted fights and disagreements. If you are a woman with these characteristics, then pray unto the Most High God with a sincere heart that he heals you and allows you to walk in the ways of the virtuous woman or wife you are called to be.

---

**Proverbs 30:20 Such is the way of an adulterous woman; she eateth, and wipeth her mouth, and saith, I have done no wickedness.**

**Adulterous—**Voluntary sexual intercourse between a married man or woman and a partner other than the legal spouse.

Stay away from an adulterous woman, for she is wicked. Please don't get caught up in the snares of this woman for she will lead you to destruction. If you are a woman who is battling with this, pray unto the Most High God with a sincere heart, asking him to give you deliverance of that evil spirit that's upon you. Pray, day and night, for deliverance, for he loves those that love him.

---

**2 Esdras 16:49 Like as a whore envieth a right honest and virtuous woman** – *Authorized KJV Apocrypha*

**Whore**— To be or act as a prostitute.

Please stay away from a whore, for she will have envy in her heart towards a virtuous woman who is walking in the ways of the Most High God. As a man, be caution of the women you are around, for evil spirits will get you to stray away from those who are seeking righteousness.

---

**Ecclesiasticus 9:3 Meet not with an harlot, lest thou fall into her snares.** – *Authorized KJV Apocrypha*

**Harlot**— A prostitute or promiscuous woman.

**Snares**— To catch or trap in or as if in a snare; capture by trickery.

Men, please stay away from a prostitute (harlot) for she has many tricks to deceive you. Some men have died dealing with this type of wicked and evil woman. If you are a woman who is a prostitute or knows someone who is, then pray for them, sincerely from the heart, and hope that the Most High God will give them a chance to repent.

**Ecclesiasticus 25:16-23 I had rather dwell with a lion and a dragon, than to keep house with a wicked woman. The wickedness of a woman changeth her face, and darkeneth her countenance like sackcloth. Her husband shall sit among his neighbours; and when he heareth it shall sigh bitterly. All wickedness is but little to the wickedness of a woman: let the portion of a sinner fall upon her. As the climbing up a sandy way is to the feet of the aged, so is a wife full of words to a quiet man. Stumble not at the beauty of a woman, and desire her not for pleasure. A woman, if she maintain her husband, is full of anger, impudence, and much reproach. A wicked woman abateth the courage, maketh an heavy countenance and a wounded heart: a woman**

that will not comfort her husband in distress maketh weak hands and feeble knees. – *Authorized KJV Apocrypha*

Men please stay away from a wicked woman for she changes her face and her appearance, meaning what she wears will be dark to resemble who she is inside. Repent and pray to the Most High God that he leads you away from sin and dealing with these types of women. Women, repent and pray if you are dealing with these problems.

---

**Ecclesiasticus 26:6-7 But a grief of heart and sorrow is a woman that is jealous over another woman, and a scourge of the tongue which communicateth with all. An evil wife is a yoke shaken to and fro: he that hath hold of her is as though he held a scorpion.** – *Authorized KJV Apocrypha*

**Jealous—** Resentful (of) or vindictive (towards), especially through envy.

Men, stay away from a jealous woman. This type of woman will cause all types of arguments for no reason. If you are a woman who is jealous, please pray to the Most High God that he removes this nasty spirit out of you, because Satan can come into your heart and change you to be a woman that is evil and wicked. Men, pray unto the Most High God that you will not meet a woman like this.

---

**Ecclesiasticus 26:8-9 A drunken woman and a gadder abroad causeth great anger, and she will not cover her own shame. The whoredom of a woman may be known in her haughty looks and eyelids.** – *Authorized KJV Apocrypha*

**Drunken—** Intoxicated with or as if with alcohol.

# MEN

**Gadder—** To go out in search of pleasure, especially in an aimless manner; gallivant.

Men, please stay away from a woman who likes to get drunk all the time and a woman who likes to have sex. Also, the whoredom of a woman may be known in her appearance and eyelids. If you are a woman who fits these characteristics, then repent and pray unto the Most High God for deliverance out of your situation and he will bring it to pass. Men pray for them as well.

---

**Ecclesiasticus 26:25 A shameless woman shall be counted as a dog; but she that is shamefaced will fear the Lord.** – *Authorized KJV Apocrypha*

**Shameless—** Done without shame; without decency or modesty.

**Dog—** An unattractive or boring girl or woman.

Men, stay away from a shameless woman, for she will cause you more trouble than good. Go after a woman who is shamefaced before the Most High God.

---

**1 Esdras 4:22-27 By this also ye must know that women have dominion over you: do ye not labour and toil, and give and bring all to the woman? Yea, a man taketh his sword, and goeth his way to rob and to steal, to sail upon the sea and upon rivers; And looketh upon a lion, and goeth in the darkness; and when he hath stolen, spoiled, and robbed, he bringeth it to his love. Wherefore a man loveth his wife better than father or mother. Yea, many there be that have run out of their wits for women, and become servants for their sakes. Many also**

**have perished, have erred, and sinned, for women.** – *Authorized KJV Apocrypha*

**Wits**— The mind or memory.

These scriptures say it all: Men have lost their minds over women. Men must follow the Words of the Most High God for guidance and instructions. Many men have perished, erred, sinned, and done foolish things for women. Just look at King David for an example. Pray to the Most High God that you be not taken in at the beauty of a woman, but remember to try the spirit.

# Notes

# Women

Women can easily get caught up in their emotions, thus causing them to make the wrong choice in a man. If you are a woman who proclaims to love the Most High God, then pray unto him, day and night, asking the Father to send the man that is ordained for you, if that's the Most High God's will. Please women, guide and bring your daughters up in the Word of the Most High God for his Words are faithful and true. Humble yourself as a woman by not walking in pride, but walking shamefaced before the Most High God asking him to guide you and to keep you from wicked men. Women, please know that you are the weaker vessel.

**Proverbs 14:7 Go from the presence of a foolish man, when thou perceivest not in him the lips of knowledge.**

**Foolish—** Unwise; silly.

Women, please stay away from a foolish man for he will cause you great trouble. Men who are foolish, repent and desire wisdom from the Most High God so you don't allow the enemy to use you as a tool to destroy and mislead women.

# WOMEN

**Proverbs 16:28 A froward man soweth strife: and a whisperer separateth chief friends.**

**Froward**— Obstinate; contrary.

**Strife**— Angry or violent struggle; conflict.

Stay away from a man who is stubborn and who is headstrong about what he says, for he will stir up unwanted conflicts for no reason. Men, if you have these characteristics in you, humble yourself and pray to the Most High God that He removes that spirit out of you.

**Proverbs 16:29 A violent man enticeth his neighbour, and leadeth him into the way that is not good.**

**Violent**— (of a person) tending to the use of violence, especially in order to injure or intimidate others.

Women stay away from a man who is violent; if you see these signs then please remove yourself from the situation so you won't become another victim of domestic violence. The Most High God knows best for you as his child. Men, learn to humble yourself and have control over yourself and pray that the Most High God enables you to walk in his ways.

---

**Proverbs 22:24 Make no friendship with an angry man; and with a furious man thou shalt not go.**

**Angry**— Feeling or expressing annoyance, animosity, or resentment; enraged.

Women, don't be friends with a man who is quick to anger, for he will cause you trouble. Please don't even bother to make friends with him, nor be lured in by his smooth talk or appearance. Men, humble yourself in the sight of the Most High God and repent so you can be that man or husband that the Most High God has called you to be.

---

**Proverbs 29:23 A man's pride shall bring him low: but honour shall uphold the humble in spirit.**

**Pride—** (1) A feeling of honour and self-respect; a sense of personal worth. (2) Excessive self-esteem; conceit.

Please stay away from a man who is prideful, because sooner or later the Most High God will bring him low. If you are a man who is prideful, please ask the Most High God to humble you and allow you to shine like the light you are called to be.

---

**Ecclesiasticus 11:29 Bring not every man into thine house: for the deceitful man hath many trains.** – *Authorized KJV Apocrypha*

**Trains—** To control or guide towards a specific goal.

Women must be cautions of a deceitful man, for he has the goal to entrap you by various means. If you are a woman, please pray unto the Most High God for guidance and protection so you won't be lead to one of these types of men.

---

# WOMEN

**Ecclesiasticus 11:33 Take heed of a mischievous man, for he worketh wickedness; lest he bring upon thee a perpetual blot.** – *Authorized KJV Apocrypha*

**Mischievous—** Teasing; slightly malicious.

Women, stay away from a man who likes to play and act silly all the time for he has wickedness in him. Be very careful lest you fall into his snares. Women, pray without ceasing because you are the weaker vessel.

---

**Ecclesiasticus 14:8 The envious man hath a wicked eye; he turneth away his face, and despiseth men.** – *Authorized KJV Apocrypha*

**Envious—** (1) A feeling of grudging or somewhat admiring discontent aroused by the possessions, achievements, or qualities of another. (2) The desire to have for oneself something possessed by another; covetousness.

Please stay far away from an envious man, for he has a wicked eye. How can a man love you if he is envious of others for no reason? Sooner or later he will envy you. If you are a man who is envious of someone, please repent of your sins and pray unto the Most High God for deliverance. Women, if your husband shows these signs, pray unto the Most High God that he changes his ways.

---

**Ecclesiasticus 14:9 A covetous man's eye is not satisfied with his portion; and the iniquity of the wicked drieth up his soul.** – *Authorized KJV Apocrypha*

**Covetous—** Jealously eager for the possession of something (especially the property of another person).

Stay away from a covetous man for he is never satisfied with what he has. These type of men will suck you dry; they will use you and leave you emotionally broken. If you are a man who struggles with this spirit, pray unto the Most High God, day and night, and ask the Father to forgive you of your sin. You must repent with a sincere heart.

---

**Ecclesiasticus 22:1-2 A slothful man is compared to a filthy stone, and every one will hiss him out to his disgrace. 2 A slothful man is compared to the filth of a dunghill: every man that takes it up will shake his hand.** – *Authorized KJV Apocrypha*

**Slothful**— Disliking work or effort; lazy; idle.

Please stay far away from a lazy man. He will bring more grief into your life than good. Women, please don't make excuses for your husband if he is like this, because you will find yourself very unhappy. A man is supposed to be the provider of the household. Don't make excuses for a man who is just plain lazy and doesn't want to do anything, instead pray for that man.

---

**Ecclesiasticus 23:11 A man that useth much swearing shall be filled with iniquity, and the plague shall never depart from his house: if he shall offend, his sin shall be upon him: and if he acknowledge not his sin, he maketh a double offence: and if he swear in vain, he shall not be innocent, but his house shall be full of calamities.** – *Authorized KJV Apocrypha*

**Swearing**— To give evidence or make any statement or solemn declaration on oath.

# WOMEN

Be very careful of a man that promises you things and doesn't do what he says, for you are being deceived. Men like this get women on an emotional high and then they break them down. Also, this is how women become bitter and angry for choosing the wrong man. Women, pray that the Most High God sends a man who is made for you.

---

**Ecclesiasticus 23:16-19 Two sorts of men multiply sin, and the third will bring wrath: a hot mind is as a burning fire, it will never be quenched till it be consumed: a fornicator in the body of his flesh will never cease till he hath kindled a fire. All bread is sweet to a whoremonger, he will not leave off till he die. A man that breaketh wedlock, saying thus in his heart, Who seeth me? I am compassed about with darkness, the walls cover me, and no body seeth me; what need I to fear? the Most High will not remember my sins: Such a man only feareth the eyes of men, and knoweth not that the eyes of the Most High are ten thousand times brighter than the sun, beholding all the ways of men, and considering the most secret parts.** – *Authorized KJV Apocrypha*

**Fornicator—** To indulge in or commit fornication.

**Whoremonger—** A person who consorts with whores; lecher.

**Wedlock—** Born out of wedlock born when one's parents are not legally married.

Women, stay far away from a fornicator, a whoremonger, and a man who has a child out of wedlock. These types of men are wicked and will cause you to err. Also, these types of men will destroy your soul. If you know men like this, pray unto the Most High God that he changes their ways to serve him so that they can walk in the spirit and not fulfill the lust of their flesh. If you are a man like this, then stop and repent. Doing such acts doesn't make you a man, it makes you a sinner marked for death.

---

**Ecclesiasticus 40:28-30 My son, lead not a beggar's life; for better it is to die than to beg. The life of him that dependeth on another man's table is not to be counted for a life; for he polluteth himself with other men's meat: but a wise man well nurtured will beware thereof. Begging is sweet in the mouth of the shameless: but in his belly there shall burn a fire.** – *Authorized KJV Apocrypha*

**Beggar**— A person who begs, especially one who lives by begging.

Please don't deal with a man who likes to beg. For the Word says it is better to die than beg. So, if you know someone like this, pray that the Most High God deliver them from this spirit and allow them to work with their own hands and not have to beg to another man.

# Notes

# Afterword

Let nothing discourage you, for the Most High God has not given us a spirit of fear or cowardice, but a spirit of power, and love, and of a sound mind. Remember to walk by faith and humble yourself, trusting in the Most High God at all times with your whole heart, knowing he will bring anything to pass to those that love him.

**For God hath not given us the spirit of fear; but of power, and of love, and of a sound mind.**

**2 Timothy 1:7**

# Bibliography

*The Holy Bible.* Authorized King James Version Pure Cambridge Edition *KJV Apocrypha.* Cambridge: Cambridge UP, 1983. Print.

*Collins English Dictionary*—Complete & Unabridged 10th Edition.

www.ingramcontent.com/pod-product-compliance
Lightning Source LLC
Chambersburg PA
CBHW021411290426
44108CB00010B/479